Living WESTERN HORSEMANSHIP

Personal Narratives by
LEADING HORSEMEN OF THE AMERICAN WEST

EDITED BY TAMMY LEROY

PHOTOGRAPHS BY ROBERT DAWSON

THE LYONS PRESS
Guilford, Connecticut
An imprint of The Globe Pequot Press

The Lyons Press is an imprint of The Globe Pequot Press

10 9 8 7 6 5 4 3 2 1

Printed in China
Designed by Bryan E. Daws, D2 Design Communication Design Studio

ISBN 978-1-59921-253-1

Library of Congress Cataloging-in-Publication Data is available on file.

THIS BOOK IS DEDICATED
TO THE HALF MILLION YOUNG MEMBERS
OF THE
NATIONAL FFA ORGANIZATION.

Advisor and teacher Dave Yost and his students from the Joseph, Oregon,

chapter of the FFA; FFA supporters Brent and Connie McKinley;

and the nine contributing writers who care about the future

of America's youth made this book possible.

Thank you to Tammy LeRoy, Robert Dawson, Bryan Daws and Katy Jane Bothum

for their contribution to this project. With the help of Kathryn Mennone

and Maureen Graney of The Lyons Press, a portion of the proceeds from this book

will go to the National FFA Organization.

"The FFA is a big part in the foundation of this country.
Established in 1928, the commitment, responsibility, ethics and goals that it teaches
our youth is tremendous. This organization is making a positive difference
in these young men and women's lives. Horsemanship also stems from this great organization
and I am proud to have been able to help FFA so that it can carry on
with its work for future generations to come."
– Chris Cox

Contents

Foreword

From the time horses were first brought to North America by the Spanish in the 16th century, the people of the American West have sought to tame, perfect, and understand the magnificent creature we call the horse. Throughout each century, a handful of individuals have emerged who possess exceptional horsemanship abilities. Today, as in the past, others have flocked toward these gifted men and women who serve as teachers and mentors to all who seek to better understand these animals. Those who have contributed to this book are indeed among the extraordinary horsemen of our time.

Their names comprise a Who's Who of western horsemanship. Some are retired from celebrated careers in which they've made their indelible marks on the industry; others, although already legendary in stature, are in their primes with decades more to contribute to the world of western horsemanship.

All of these individuals have been influential in the industry and most have shared their expertise with the horse world through books, training videos, clinics, and workshops. Through these means, their audiences can gather a wealth of training information and can learn the techniques of good horsemanship from the masters of the trade—everything from starting a young colt to high-level performance moves on cutting horses. In this book, however, these celebrated horsemen offer an altogether different type of instruction.

Along with their extensive knowledge of ways to get maximum performance from a horse, each of these men through their years of experience has come to possess priceless wisdom about the nature of the horse and its relationship with man. Through this special connection, each has learned also a great deal about the art of living. It is this insight and understanding they share in *Living Western Horsemanship: Personal Narratives by Leading Horsemen of the American West*, and their words are highlighted by Robert Dawson's stirring photos.

While each writer has his own unique philosophies and wisdom to convey, among their similarities are a love for the western lifestyle and a tireless work ethic. Though they are horsemen, the lessons they impart hold value for individuals of any age and from any walk of life who aspire to higher standards and an enriched life.

Known as the "Father of the Cutting Horse," Buster Welch's influence on the cutting industry cannot be overemphasized. He is a legend in every sense of the word. Buster's guileless and humorous style almost makes one forget that he is a five-time NCHA Open Futurity Champion, a four-time NCHA Open World Champion, and a member of several prestigious halls of fame.

In addition to holding his much-acclaimed clinics on basic to advanced horsemanship, colt starting, ranch and cattle work, problem-solving, reining, and trail obstacles, Craig Cameron has produced eight successful videos as well as a best-selling book. His writing reflects not only his love for working with horses but also his devotion to preserving the values and moral code of the old-time cowboys.

Al Dunning has been recognized as a national and local leader in the Quarter Horse and Reining world for over thirty years. He and his students have earned twenty-one world titles, including nine AQHA World Championships. A true horseman, Al says, is a person who understands what is going on with a horse beyond the obvious. His inspiring tales of remarkable horses he has worked with make his essay one to be treasured.

A sincere respect and keen understanding of the horse are at the heart of John Lyons' phenomenal career as a trainer and clinician. For over twenty-five years, he has taught students from beginners to upper-level performance how to get the most out of their relationships with their horses. The insights into horsemanship he shares in his essay will cause even the most experienced horseman or horsewoman to walk away with a better understanding of the creature John calls "God's favorite animal."

Known in the industry as "the trainer's trainer," Bob Avila has earned more than thirty-seven world championship and reserve titles during a successful career spanning thirty-five years, competing in events from performance to halter. Bob believes the keys to success in horsemanship are to love what you are doing, believe in yourself, and believe in your product, which is the end result of your committed efforts.

Two things stand out most about Leon Harrel, a two-time winner of the National Cutting Horse Association Futurity and a respected trainer and teacher. One is his dogged dedication to non-violent treatment of horses, which springs from his deep love for the animal; the other is his lively enthusiasm for the cutting horse industry.

Ron Ralls' background of running a ranch for nearly three decades before entering the show world has given his training style a distinctive, authentic quality. A renowned reined cow horse competitor, he is a two-time winner of the World's Greatest Horseman Contest. As he eloquently expresses in his essay, Ron believes a good horseman must be fair, open-minded, and always ready to learn something new.

The brilliant career of seven-time World Champion team roper Jake Barnes provides a classic example of how hard work, determination, and faith lead to success. A winner of the prestigious Legends of ProRodeo Award in 2006, Jake was honored for exemplary character and leadership in the home, the arena, and the community.

Ronnie Richards has enjoyed a wonderfully successful career both as a competitor and a world-class trainer; nevertheless, he says he hopes to be remembered as a great horseman rather than a great competitor. Ronnie's stories of "hopeless" horses he has helped transform into champions serve as inspiration to anyone who has ever believed in the unseen potential that lies both in horses and in people.

The last section of this book is a tribute to Ray Hunt, a living legend in the horse world. His well-known precept, "Make the wrong thing hard and the right thing easy," is embraced by many of today's top trainers. In fact, so many of the horse industry's most successful trainers have been influenced by Ray's wisdom that it is no exaggeration to say that the pervasive philosophy embraced in western horsemanship today is a result of his inspired teachings.

By any standards, the contributors to this book are extraordinary men. These living legends of western horsemanship serve as inspirations not only to horsemen and horsewomen of all disciplines, but to anyone who has a desire to live a life of accomplishment, integrity, and higher purpose.

Tammy LeRoy
Editor

Buster Welch, known as the Father of the Cutting Horse, has dedicated his life to enhancing
the cutting horse industry. He is a five-time NCHA Open Futurity Champion and a four-time
NCHA Open World Champion, winning four World Championships with Marion's Girl in the 1950s,
and with Mr. San Peppy in the 1970s.

Buster's hall of fame inductions include the American Quarter Horse Association Hall of Fame;
National Cutting Horse Association Hall of Fame; National Cutting Horse Association Riders Hall of Fame;
and Texas Cowboy Hall of Fame. He is also the recipient of the American Cowboy Culture Working Cowboy Award;
Charles Goodnight Award; Foy Proctor Memorial Cowman's Award of Honor;
and the Zane Schulte Trainer of the Year.

With all of his accolades as a cutting horse champion, Buster has made it no secret that he considers
himself a rancher first and foremost. Today he works cattle and holds a partnership on the Double Mountain
River Ranch near Rotan, Texas, with his wife, Sheila, who is also a cutting horse champion.

COWBOYS, CUTTING HORSES, AND OTHER GOOD TIMES

Buster Welch

The horse is about as noble an animal as I ever fooled with, and good ones have as much dignity or more so as any other creature. Horses are extremely intelligent; if you don't think they are, just try to match wits with them! I have a theory that man never started to develop his brain or his nobility until he got a'horseback. The man on horseback had time to think, to go see more things, and to understand more. His genes are probably the ones that survived, so that gene is in everybody. You never stood on the street and saw a good-looking horse come by that everyone didn't look.

I was raised by my grandparents in my early years and I spent most of my time tagging along with cowboys who moved livestock. They would always gather around a cutting horse called Old Snip and brag about the outstanding things they'd seen him do—jump a bush to head a cow, jump backward, or some unusual thing. I must have been younger than four years old when I started riding him because I can remember going to my grandmother after I'd been a'horseback on my fourth birthday and asking her when I was going to grow. I had it in my mind that every year on your birthday you spurted up several inches, and I couldn't feel myself growing. I wanted to get bigger so I could do more with the cowboys.

A lot of times when we were penning one of the cowboys would turn a cow back into me just to watch that old horse head 'er—and me having a hard time staying on. I think that appealed to my ego, and it also caused me to respect and appreciate a good horse. Old Snip was just a real good cow horse. He was what they called a "steeldust" in that day, which was a forerunner of the Quarter Horse. I'd drive a jackrabbit up against a sheep-proof fence sometimes and

8

hold it three or four turns before it'd get away. We didn't have as many horses with "cow" back then; but boy, there were some good ones!

The cow horse goes plumb back to B.C., and ever since people have been handling livestock on horseback, there have been outstanding cow horses. I was raised around people who thought the horse was a tool and a method, but I loved horses. They gave me freedom. I love the old Spanish saying that a man without a horse is a man without feet, and that was especially true in the country I grew up in.

Automobiles weren't too useful where I was raised. I can remember that if it rained, I'd sit with my grandmother on the front porch listening to people who were stuck and she'd guess who it was by the sound of their motors even though they might be four or five miles away. You hear people say "fixin" to go somewhere. I think where that came from is, if we were going to go to town on Saturday, we'd start fixin' on Friday. We'd get the Model T out, close the spigot, fill it with water, and patch a tire or two. It was a long distance to get anywhere, but I could get on horseback and just go.

EARLY DAYS AS A COWBOY

I later moved to Midland with my dad and his new wife, and they put me in school. My mother had died when I was three weeks old and I had lived with my grandparents until that point. Cowboys driving their herds would come right by the school on the way to the stock pens, and I could hardly stand to see those cowboys out there on horseback! When the war started, everybody was short-handed and working around the clock, so I started day working because the ranchers were short of help. I had run off from home a time or two before; but when I finally ran off and went to work for Foy and Leonard Procter, my family just left me alone. I could make as much as a grown man and I wanted to be a rancher; I didn't realize then how much I needed school.

My job was breaking young horses and doing the jobs that didn't take a lot of skill to relieve a skilled man from doing those jobs. One of my chores was gathering and cutting firewood for camp. I didn't realize my name wasn't "Get Wood" until I was seventeen years old. When we were

working the roundups, I had the boring job of holding the cuts, but it was a wonderful place to observe good men working cattle.

The biggest cattle roundup I was ever on was at the Four Sixes. They had sold two thousand cows with a guarantee of sixty percent calf crop to go to Wyoming, and we gathered all summer and threw them into traps. We were going to bring them up and cut out the shippers. We drove those cows for several days to Ash Creek Trails and I believe to Yellow Horse Trap close to Guthrie, which was around fifteen sections. Some of the sub-bosses told me there were 3,500 cows in the roundup. We started on the south side of the ranch and came plumb up to Guthrie.

We would gather at Yellow Horse Trap early in the morning and throw the cattle out on the roundup ground. We would cut out the cows and calves they wanted to keep. After about four hours, they quit mammying up and we would have to graze and water them and throw them back into the trap for the night. It took about four days to cut out the 1,500 keeping cattle. Then, just as we were ready to drive the shipping cattle to put them on the train, John L. Lewis—the head of the railroad union—called a strike.

Of course, there was no grass left in Yellow Horse Trap. We'd have to gather them every morning and take them to Ash Creek Pasture, which was 50,000 acres, hold them and graze them all day, and throw them back in the trap at night. We had to day herd the cattle this way for about a week, but seemed like forever. I was riding the rough string, and not getting to blow them out on the drive made them want to buck. It was tough going.

Once I was working up on James Kinney's ranch in the Guadalupe Mountains in New Mexico. We had around five hundred Brahma cows and we were branding calves. They came from Florida, and had been worked with dogs but never with horses. We were about a quarter-mile from the highway getting ready to do some branding. We were very cautious for awhile, but the cows seemed to have settled down. James left four cowboys holding the roundup and put the rest of us afoot for a branding crew. We tied our horses up to the southwest of the herd and started branding.

A photographer saw us from the road and stopped about two hundred yards from the herd to take pictures. He took a picture or two, and then squatted down to take another one.

All of a sudden, every cow was on her feet in a dead run like someone had shot a rifle. I remember being afoot and it was the funniest thing just to hear those cattle crack and go into a dead run. The cattle broke to the southeast, and there were a lot of wrecks with cowboys trying to get to their horses and get on. It was quite a scramble.

One guy was running beside me when his horse ran backward, broke loose, and fell over; I could see him trying to get on the horse while he was down. We went about three quarters of a mile before we got them stopped. About fourteen of them fell into a canyon and were brought back later. It was quite an adventure.

LOOKING FOR COW HORSES

Out of every group of horses I'd break, I'd save myself two or three good cutting horses. My job was to relieve good cowboys and hold the cut. Foy and Leonard were good horsemen. I noticed they could drive their cattle straight out of that herd and straight to the cut no matter how hard the cattle tried to get back. Everyone else who was cutting would do a lot of running. I got to watching Foy and Leonard and noticed their horses would stop real straight. And when they'd turn around, they'd crack over their hocks and it wouldn't scare a cow. So I started doing that on my broncs and that started me out with that style. I think I was the first cutter who ran straight and stopped when showing cutting horses.

I was real fortunate to get Chickasha Mike, and even more fortunate to get Marion's Girl. Her mother was out of a Tallwood, who was a government remount stud. Prior to World War I, the Germans came to the U.S. and bought all the good cavalry horses they could; so when the war started, we were short of good horses. The government started a remount program and a lot of the Thoroughbred breeders donated studs. Among those was a Triple Crown winner. When a rancher signed up for a stud, if he was approved, I think he had to let his neighbors breed for five dollars a mare. The government had first option to buy any geldings that went up for sale.

I think the remount horses did much to improve ranch horses in America, and they were sure enough cow horses. Marion's Girl was out of a Tallwood mare and by a son of Wimpy from the King Ranch. He was full of cow. There are a lot of horses with cow bred in them now, but back in my day, you'd be lucky if you were raising horses and ten percent of them would watch a cow.

They were holding cutting contests as far back as the 1800s, but during the Depression in the 1920s, they quit having them. The contests started again in Stamford in 1933, and the Cutting Horse Association was formed in 1946 at the Fort Worth Stock Show.

I was breaking some colts for Homer Ingram in Las Vegas, New Mexico, and there was an older colt out that had had a bad start and had outlawed. I had to put some time in on him but I noticed he was just full of cow. I tried to buy him but Homer said, "I won't sell him, but that stud he's out of is getting kin to too many of my mares, so I'll sell you him." The stud, Chickasha Mike, had his own band of mares he ran with. I bought Chickasha Mike range-delivered!

THE CUTTING HORSE FUTURITY

There were about ten of us who underwrote the first futurity—myself, Charlie Boyd, and eight other Sweetwater businessmen. We had to do something to get the sport going again because cutting horses were dying out. My contribution was $250. I won the first futurity on Money's Glo, and he was sure enough a good little cow horse.

It was a real thrill, but we didn't know whether they would even have another one. I won $3,700, and you could buy a loaded four-door Mercury back then for that money! We lost $2,500 that first year, but the next year, the futurity made money. I won the next year too and it paid even more. I ended up winning the NCHA Futurity five times over the years.

I think we've been very fortunate to have the finest people running the association and good people involved in cutting horses. I think it's been a roaring success, My personal aim when we started the futurity was to borrow from the car industry and force a need for a new horse every year to encourage breeding and training, which was going to nothing. The industry has succeeded better than any of us ever dreamed.

Of course, you can always find something wrong to criticize. I'm a little bit like Winston Churchill who said, "Any damned fool can see what's wrong. It takes a smart man to see what's right!" I can see some things wrong in the industry, but I've noticed that they have a way of righting themselves. In nearly every futurity I've seen—and I've seen all of them—I think we've come damned near getting the right horse winning it. I think that's remarkable.

A guy training for the futurity doesn't have much time to go into other things, and there's no question that sometimes, some of these horses are used a little hard. Most of them go into stud or are bred, which has really accentuated the cow in our horses. Things aren't perfect in the industry, but there are so many things going right. The most wonderful thing about cutting is that it's so wholesome and so American. There are many levels, and there is a place for nearly everybody. It's a big tent.

I spent a lot of time trying to help get the cutting industry going to where a cowboy could make a living at it. I believe there are more good skilled cowboys today and more good horses; good horses make good horsemen. There are a lot of good horsemen who never get a chance to sing their songs because they never get that one outstanding horse.

When I was training, I liked to think I was more responsible than I was but I think it's probably seventy percent about the horse and thirty percent about the trainer. An outstanding horse makes a better trainer quicker than an outstanding trainer makes a better horse.

LOOKING AHEAD

The ranching industry is certainly seeing some changes. There is some land that's not very good for anything but grazing cattle, but there are some hunters and Ted Turners out there who are buying up land and taking it out of production. That's going to affect the ranching industry. In truth, there's still a lot of land and cattle, and a lot of need for a cowboy. I see the ranching industry continuing, but I guess I've always been optimistic. Somebody once said that you ought to stick with an optimistic guy because it's going to be bad enough if he's right!

I often say I left home with an uncluttered mind—which is my way of saying I didn't have an education! That doesn't mean that I think not getting an education is the thing to do. I would love to have had a good education. I bought a one-way ticket to cowboying and ranching and I had to make it, but I never quit trying to educate myself. I was lucky to have worked for some smart people who read and who were

interesting to listen to. I've always loved to read. The old bunkhouses were papered with old newspapers, and I'd read them all.

Today we're competing with China, India, and the rest of the world and we've got to stay competitive. I always told my children to cowboy and ride bucking horses for fun, but get an education and learn to work at something else to make a

living. I never felt right about just training horses to make a living so I kept ranching. I was raised a working cowboy and always felt I should do something to produce.

I feel I've had a pretty good career, but your creative ability will always be passed by your creative sensibility. You'll always look back and see how you could have done it better. That's the seed that keeps you riding those horses!

I have a theory that man never started to develop his brain or his nobility until

They gave me freedom. I love the old Spanish saying that a man without a hor

...got a horseback. The man on horseback had time to think, to go see more things,

...is a man without feet, and that was especially true in the country I grew up in.

Native Texan Craig Cameron is one of the original clinicians, and he is on the road forty-four weeks each year demonstrating the style of horsemanship he has perfected for over twenty years. Called the "public defender of the horse," Craig dedicates himself to those who educate their horses by first educating themselves. At an age where most have long since retired the thought of starting colts, Craig starts hundreds of horses each year as well as holding four-day clinics at his ranches in Bluff Dale, Texas, and Lincoln, New Mexico, where he blends education with entertainment.

His clinic topics range from basic to advanced horsemanship, colt starting, ranch and cattle work, problem-solving, reining, and trail obstacles. He has produced eight successful videos as well as a best-selling book.

Craig's humility and fairness go a long way with both horses and people, and by using the western way of life so successfully in his endeavor to teach and communicate his skills, Craig is keeping our western heritage alive.

PRESERVING THE COWBOY WAY

Craig Cameron

Horsemanship is really an art form. It takes almost a lifetime to become great at it, and there are always new goals to reach along the way. My goal today is to develop what I call the "brave horse." The brave horse will go anywhere and do anything you want, because he trusts you. Trust is a belief, and you don't want to destroy the horse's belief that you would never do anything to hurt or harm him. To do this, you must learn how to use what I call your five "senses:" sensibility, sensitivity, common sense, horse sense—and don't forget your sense of humor! When you do this right, it looks like magic. It isn't. It's a commonsense approach that we sometimes call "horse sense."

FIFTY MILLION YEARS OF INSTINCT

I'm not sure if you can say that the relationship between man and horse is a natural one. They say the horse is fifty million years old, and man's first dealing with them was to kill them for food. We, as humans, have a predator mentality, while the horse has a prey mentality. We should not take it for granted, then, when this amazing prey animal allows the predator to get right up on its back. This is so unnatural for them that it's amazing the horse will accept it. He accepts it when he comes to believe that you're not going to hurt him. For this reason, you should not work with a horse through pain and fear. If you use that approach, the only response you will get from the horse is instinct.

Of course, some people do a better job than others at gaining a horse's trust, and some horses have a stronger impulse toward self-preservation. You can't take the instinct away, so you must work with him in a way that allows him to figure out that he doesn't have to use his instinct. Training is development through gradually increasing demands. If you push too hard, the horse will respond with the instinct that is fifty million years old. Sometimes, the best strategy is simply to back off and go slow. That is the place where the horse gentles and begins to accept your leadership. Give a horse time to think.

Horsemanship is a thinking man's game. You have to outthink the horse. When a horse is doing something we consider wrong, he is only doing what he thinks he's supposed to do. It's our job to give him the reason to change. When he does the right thing, we have to give him the relief, the reward, the pet on the neck—something to let the horse know he's doing right. Half the secret to horsemanship is working with the horse instead of against the horse. We can't get excited. We can't get mad. Mad only gets in your way, and when you're mad, you're not thinking.

The herd instinct is very strong. The horse quickly figures out whether you are leading or following. He figures out whether you're an alpha or a beta. If you won't take that leadership role, then he will. He may be walking around when you try to get on. He may buck you off a time or two, and these behaviors, if they go unchecked, become habits. When you allow that to happen, you must be careful what kind of monster you are creating!

NO ROOM FOR EGO

You must take a leadership role, but a true horseman doesn't work through pain or fear; they work through understanding. I embrace Ray Hunt's philosophy of making the wrong thing difficult and making the right thing easy. How can there be a better philosophy? Your way of working with a horse may be different than mine, but you can use this philosophy. Not only does it apply to horses, it's the best philosophy for dealing with kids, dogs, and everyone else as well. Work with the correct attitude and let your idea become their idea. People are tougher to teach than horses because we let pride

and ego become involved. If you let go of your ego, you won't be dealing with a horse as if you are better than him. The horse makes you prove yourself over and over again, but he never lets you down if you are effective at presenting what you want in the right way. Then, he'll come across for you.

Of course, a horse's individual disposition also comes into play. Disposition is his ability to relate to or accept the training. Some horses certainly do that better than others, and we must always be patient with them. Patience is waiting without worry. Your job is to give the horse a reason to change, because we are stepping into his world, and we are asking something of him. In truth, the horse is perfect by nature when untouched by man. He only has a problem when we get involved. People often train horses as if the horse should know what they want, which causes both the horse and the person to get frustrated. It's our job to teach the horse, so the real question is: how good of a job are you doing getting the horse to understand what you want? Truly, that ability is the making of a horseman.

As long as the horse is relaxed, comfortable, and understands, you are doing alright. But if he is none of those things, then it is you who must be willing to change. People often try to make changes through pride or through ego, but the horse never works through ego. That's one of his most beautiful traits. You won't hurt his pride because a horse does not work through foolish pride. He is willing to accept leadership. Sometimes he will vie you for it; but if you prove your leadership, he will accept it.

THE POWER OF UNDERSTANDING

I grew up in the 1950s in Texas, spending a lot of my time on ranches. All I ever wanted was to be a cowboy, so I really looked up to the old-time cowboys I was around. But even as a kid, I would watch the rough way some men handled horses, and I knew it wasn't right. Fortunately, there have always been great horsemen. The man who first influenced me a great deal was Ray Hunt. I went to several Ray Hunt clinics, and was influenced by his ideas on working through the power of understanding. Later, I began to talk with Tom Dorrance, and he was the kind of man who would make you work for the answers.

As I go further down the road, I can see that all great horsemen have worked through the power of understanding. Understanding doesn't mean there isn't a

time to be firm with a horse, but there's a difference between punishment and discipline. Whether it's with a horse, a dog, or your children, discipline is an art form. Discipline has a different effect on the horse than punishment—he's not scared, he's not hurt, and he doesn't develop fear or resentment. Discipline, when done correctly, has a positive effect on the horse.

Every day with a horse is a new beginning. From good beginnings, things come naturally. I want to have a truly good relationship with my horse. I'm working to be just one thing, and that is a horse-man, but I also want my horse to be a man-horse. To be a horseman, you must learn to read a horse—his eyes, his ears, his posture, his expression— everything. That's where experience comes into play. It really boils down to communication. In fact, teaching is the art of communication, and true communication is two minds listening and two minds open.

The Cowboy Way

When I was young, during the summers I lived with the Hamers—a famous Texas Ranger and ranching family. I stayed with C.P. and Harrison Hamer, who were traditional old-time cowboys. I grew up around men who were tough, and from them I learned about the "cowboy way." They taught me that a person is all about his word and his reputation. That means that if you say you're going to do something, by God, do it! If you've got a job to do, do it—even if it means staying up all night or getting up early.

I learned from these men that you either gain or lose respect every day. For me, the American West—the cowboy way— is about working for what you want. It's not about anyone giving it to you. Nobody can give you experience; you have to work at it. You can't make a great horse without working at it consistently. The horse keeps us honest in that way.

I've been working in public for over twenty years doing demonstrations. At fifty-eight years old, I am still starting literally hundreds of colts a year. These are horses I've never seen before; I don't screen them first, so I end up getting some very tough horses. People used to say to me, "Craig, aren't you scared getting on all these horses?" Now they say, "Aren't you scared getting on these horses *at your age?*" I have to stay fit to do that, so when I'm on the road, I work out in the room every night.

Giving these exhibitions, I don't just deal with the nature of the horse; I'm also dealing with the nature of the human being. The nature of the human being says, "Craig Cameron's coming to town? We've got a horse for him!" and they bring on the tough ones. To do that, I have to stay physically and mentally tough and I have to be positive.

I rode bulls for a long time, and that sport is all about positive thinking and believing in yourself. Like my friend Ty Murray says, "Never weaken." I always try to avoid the bronc ride, but sometimes you have to make one, so you have to be fit and keep a tough attitude. You don't quit; you cowboy up. A champion is not a man who never loses—a champion is a man who never quits.

I see the old cowboy way dying out, and that's what I wouldn't want us to lose. The many luxuries we now have in the horse industry have become necessities, and I don't want to see us become soft or dependent on these things. We need to still be willing to get out there and work; to go back to our roots. Cowboying is such a wonderful thing that sometimes I ask myself why anyone would want to do anything else. It's the greatest life in the world. Not so long ago, being a cowboy was about getting up every day and working the cows. That's what I like about some of the big riding outfits —the true cowboys are trying to hang on to those ways. This is what getting involved with horses does. It brings us back.

It concerns me that many of the kids today don't have a very strong work ethic, and they don't have a sense of history. Our history is essentially about being in a place where you worked for what you got, and it should be that way today. It is about having respect for your elders and still saying "Yes, sir" and "Yes, ma'am." When you say "Yes sir" to a man who deserves respect, you are also showing respect for yourself.

Everyone has a little cowboy in them. I travel a lot, and for me, the last open range is the highway. I find freedom in going from one place to the next. At times I go to live with the Crow Indians in Montana, and I like being with traditional Indians because they appreciate being close to the land and the animals. Being close to the land is an important part of getting back to our roots. In fact, the best place to ride a horse is across the countryside; I avoid working in arenas when I can.

Some of the old ways are disappearing, but as long as there are horses, there will still be a lot of cowboying going on.

Horses have much to teach us about hard work, attitude, and understanding; and sometimes, we choose to learn the hard way! The amazing thing about the horse is that, if he kicks you or bucks you off, he'll do it with no apologies and no regrets. He won't turn around and say, "Boy, I'm sorry about that." Instead, what he is trying to say is, "I've been telling you—you should have seen that coming!" When that happens, it's time to be tough, to be humble, and to work as long and as hard as necessary to reach an understanding with the horse. That is the cowboy way.

do anything you want, because he trusts you. Trust is a belief, and you don't want

his world, and we are asking something of him. In truth, the horse is perfectly

destroy the horse's belief that you would never do anything to hurt or harm him.

nature when untouched by man. He only has a problem when we get involved.

Al Dunning has served as a leader for the local and national horse industry for over thirty years. He is one of the founding members of the Arizona Quarter Horse Youth Association and its Charter President. Al also served on the USET formation committee for Reining as an Olympic sport. Since 1970, Al has owned and operated Almosta Ranch, a Quarter Horse training facility in Scottsdale, Arizona.

In 2004, Al was the recipient of the Monty Roberts Equitarian Award. In 2003, he received the Zane Schulte NCHA Trainer of the Year Award, and in 1996, Al was named American Quarter Horse Association Professional Horseman of the Year. His stunning show career includes winning the 1980 NRHA Open World Championship, the 1984 Tropicana Cutting Futurity Championship, the 1986 PCCHA Derby Championship, the1988 Las Vegas Classic/ Challenge Championship, the 1991 NCHA World Champion Open Gelding title, the 2002 NRCHA Open Bridle Horse Champion at the S.B.F., and many other major championships.

Al and his students have garnered twenty-one world titles, including nine AQHA World champions, nine AQHA Reserve World Champions, seven AQHA Amateur World Titles, numerous Arizona Year End champions, three AJQHA World Champions, and eleven All-American Congress Winners in three years.

With the AQHA, Al is a Director at Large and has served on the Show Committee for seventeen years, including Chairman of the Show Committee from 1997 to 1999. He has also served as Western Sub-Committee Chairman, and served on the Hall of Fame Committee and Nomination Credentials Committee. Al has been President of the Arizona Quarter Horse Association and the Arizona Cutting Horse Association. He has also served on Nominations, Limited Age Events, and Rules committees of the NCHA as well as National Director. In addition, Al served on the American Horse Show Association Stock Seat Committee for five years, and currently, he serves on the National Reined Cow Horse Association and AQHA judges committee.

TRUE HORSEMANSHIP

Al Dunning

I moved from Chicago to Arizona when I was eight years old. I wanted to be a cowboy, so I got together with some cowboys and started learning how to train horses. By the time I was twelve, I was riding pretty well and started showing and assisting with training. I became a professional trainer when I was twenty years old.

They say that great horses make great horse trainers. When I was only 23 years old, I had a great horse named Expensive Hobby. He is being inducted into the AQHA Hall of Fame this year. Obviously, training philosophy develops over a period of years, but I don't believe your store box of knowledge is ever full until you're done—and I'm a long way from being done.

THE BOOMERANG HORSE

Horses are amazing creatures. I'll share the story of the most resilient horse I ever worked with. Over my career, I was probably the most thrilled when I raised a horse whose mother was one of my best reining horses—a phenomenal little horse by Sugar Bars, who was one of the greats of the old-time breeding horses. Her name was Pink Pony; she was a palomino, and I loved her. I bought her in 1969 and she was one of the horses that got me really going with stock horses and reining horses. I won twenty-one straight wins on Pink Pony in reining.

Pink Pony was bred to Boon Bar, son of Doc Bar. I raised the baby, and I have to say, he wasn't very pretty. My wife named him "More Oats Please" because, with looks like his, he wasn't a horse you'd want to feed first! In fact, I gelded him early because he wasn't much to look at. He was lovable at first glance, but with a name like that, you know he had to overcome a lot.

He had an accident when he was being broke, which made him somewhat wild. He ran under a tree and cut his neck, and the wound took around seventy stitches. When he was still young and wild, I was working with him on a cow and he hit a fence, causing it to give way. When the fence came back, his foot was hung underneath. He lifted his foot, tearing it half off, including the side bone. He nearly bled to death, but the veterinarian next door was able to save him.

More Oats ended up having a terrible scar on his foot but stayed sound through these normally career-ending mishaps. Eventually, I got this horse going and he was such a phenomenal athlete that he could move very quickly. He was wild enough that he would move quickly, and sometimes, he would run away and just leave the cow!

Although it took a while, I finally got him under control and I took him to a cutting in Las Vegas where he performed fabulously. His trials weren't over, however. It had been raining in Las Vegas, and the horse slipped and ruptured

both tendons in his front legs. Fortunately, he healed, and by the time he was six years old, I qualified him for the World AQHA Show.

Still, his bad luck hadn't run out. When we were hauling him to the World Show, he was kicked by the horse next to him in the trailer. Having a wild streak, he basically went crazy. He flipped over backward, somehow getting upside down in the trailer, and the other horse stomped him and nearly killed him. His eye was nearly out of its socket because he had been thrashed around so much. I rushed him to a vet who stitched him up and saved his life once again.

It was obvious that this horse had phenomenal healing powers. I brought him home and gave him six months' rest. When I started riding him again, however, his hind legs began seeping. It was osteomyelitis, an infection that eats away at the bone. We gave him some medication that might save him, but he colicked. It looked like he was going to lose his leg and we would have to put him out of his misery. After doing all we could, we decided to simply leave him alone and see God's will for him.

Well, it shouldn't come as a surprise by now that More Oats lived and healed up completely. Since he had been through so much and kept coming back, we began to call him "The Boomerang." Two years later, I qualified him for the 1988 AQHA World Show. We drew dead last, but we won. I have to admit, I cried because of all we'd gone through and how we'd persevered. My wife and I loved that horse, and that win was pretty special to us.

That is the lesson in the story: that we had believed in him through his wildness and his many misfortunes and he eventually won the World Show. What did he have that made him special? He had heart—and, of course, some healing qualities that were unbelievable! I showed him again in 1991 and we won the NCHA Open Gelding World Championship. More Oats is still living today. He is 28 years old and taking it easy in my pasture.

We could have just given up on him and turned him out, sold him, or given him away. But I believed in that horse and I stuck with him through thick and thin, through injuries and through disappointments. You must have faith.

WINNING AND LOSING

Training horses, you feel like you know a lot at the beginning, but a lot of it is discarded as you go along. If you're trying to win and that's all it's about, some of those end up being shallow victories because you aren't always doing right by the horse. But you change your attitude eventually, and it becomes about developing the horse and not about promoting yourself.

Sometimes, people show horses that are injured or are not prepared. This can be detrimental to the horse's attitude and can reduce the length of his show career. Even though he's very talented, he hurts while he shows. Showing a horse that is in pain or is not ready is a self-centered approach, and this mindset has no place in good horsemanship.

Now I'm more sensitive of the horse's well-being and understand that this horse isn't just a vehicle to make me look good. This is a living, breathing creature that is busting his tail for me and putting out one hundred percent of his talent if I allow him to. I'm getting more out of a horse now than I ever did before.

It's really just a game of inches between winning and losing. It's really just a thread. And most winning just makes you "Champion of the Day." What I mean is that I've won a lot of blue ribbons, trophies, championships, and world championships in my career, and no one but me really cares or remembers.

So what I must do is figure out how to use my winning to benefit other people. I really try to do that. The horses I've trained thrill people—they thrill owners, they thrill audiences, and they thrill riders.

THE AMAZING CUTTING HORSE

I became well-known for reining horses after writing a book for *Western Horseman* magazine that sold over 300,000 copies. Now I focus almost entirely on cutting and working cow horses. I think it's unbelievable that a horse can do what a cutting horse does. Any kind of discipline in which we're asking them to go as fast as they can go, stop as fast as they can stop, and turn as quickly as they can turn is remarkable. All of those events seem amazing to me.

These horses are bred to cut cattle; before they're conceived, they're already working a cow. Their mother can work a cow and their father can work a cow, and these horses are bred with the dream of what they'll be able to do. Our dream is to raise the prime athlete, and then it's up to the trainer to bring that out in them.

With horses that are slow to learn, you may be saying, "I don't know if this horse has really got it." Then one day, you'll saddle him up and he'll just take hold of that cow and start working, turning, and stopping—it's like a light bulb went on! That's an amazing factor when working a cow. They don't necessarily have to show cow sense from the beginning. If we will just mold them properly and show them how to use their maximum talents, it comes pretty easily for them because they're bred for it. Young horses are astounding if you let them be. A lot of people don't let a horse do what it can do. Instead, they try to control them, and often, they inhibit them to the point that the horse can't use its talents.

TRAINING WITH CONSCIENCE

When you're young and in high gear, you go fast and you don't stop to smell the roses. You just fly by all the really good things in life. As you grow older, you shift gears, and you want things for a different reason. Instead of wanting it your way, you want to do it the right way. When you get a little older, you have the knowledge and the time to really slow down and train the way you have always wanted to. Now you can slow down and really do a great job with them.

I go through one hundred or so horses each year and I'm looking for just a few or maybe just one really great one. You'll be lucky if you find one. A lot of people will never know if they have a great horse because they won't allow the cream to come to the top.

A great horse wants to take over for you, and he wants to achieve even when you're not at your best. A great horse wants to help you in the show arena. No matter what you do outside to prepare, that horse wants to excel when you walk into that show arena. He loves the crowd. He loves the excitement. You don't have to buzz him up; he has his own adrenaline. I'm sure a lot of great horses have been overlooked or overschooled.

Training is a team effort. The horse has to want to be trained and the rider has to have a pretty good idea of what he's doing and the direction he wants to go. He has to have a goal in mind each day with the horse. And then there's patience. You go to first grade, then second grade, and then third grade. You can't just say, "Gosh he's good. I'm going to send him to high school."

Horses are like people in that there are some that have larceny in their blood. They promise you everything when you're training them, but then cheat the heck out of you when you show them. Some horses are just lazy. You know they've got it, but they just don't want to put out. Discipline can bring out their best, but that doesn't mean harsh discipline. A confident, relaxed horse will perform best.

The better the horse performs, the more he should be rewarded. I have a conscience when I'm training. I don't want to hurt an animal, but I will spank them if necessary. We're talking about a 1,200-pound horse; I don't want to get hurt. And I don't want them to hurt you if I train your horse. I want the horse to behave. I want it to know that I'm in charge and they're not. This is discipline with direction.

That said, the best horses should be rewarded with extra care. My horse, Expensive Hobby, lived to be thirty-two years old. He's buried at my place, right under his favorite tree.

THE RIGHT RELATIONSHIP

Because your horse can't talk, you have to have some type of personal relationship with him. He is relying on you entirely to take care of him, feed him, clean him, and care for his mental and physical total being. A horseman is a person with true knowledge of what is going on with the horse beyond the obvious. A true horseman can look at his horse and know what that horse is thinking, whether he is feeling happy and healthy.

Treating horses properly is like treating people properly. If I raise my voice at you, I could hurt your feelings. In the same way, if I ride a horse roughly, I can hurt his feelings also. Some people are so spiritually poor that they think a horse is a vehicle to their own happiness. But a horse is a living, feeling animal that can make you happy … but only when you think about him first.

given him away. But I believed in that horse and I stuck with him through it

think a horse is a vehicle to their own happiness. But a horse is a living, feeling

John Lyons' extraordinary ability to inspire and teach people how to become partners with their horses has launched a global training career that has spanned over twenty-five years. After a successful show career and gaining practical horse knowledge on his Colorado cattle ranch, he began giving training clinics and symposiums in 1980.

John has received much recognition in the industry. Equine Affaire chose him as the recipient of their Exceptional Equestrian Educator Award; Equitana USA chose to honor John with their highly regarded Modern Masters Award for Outstanding Horsemanship; he was winner of the University of Louisville's John W. Galbreath Award for his outstanding contributions to the horse industry; and recognized by the North American Horseman's Association for Outstanding Safety Management in the Horse Industry.

As a pioneer in the clinician movement, John has been instrumental in changing the horse industry forever. He has developed a certification program that has produced over two-hundred professional "John & Josh Lyons Certified" trainers. His Perfect Horse Magazine reaches over 150,000 monthly subscribers, and he has co-authored over twenty books and produced many video/DVDs and audio tapes. John and his wife, Jody, live in Parachute, Colorado, on Our Dream Ranch.

GOD'S FAVORITE ANIMAL

John Lyons

I teach people how to get along with their horses and train them in all different disciplines at all different levels. I work with all types of horses and mules, from beginners to problem horses to all levels of performance. In most cases, the people who come to me haven't really taken the time to think about how to break a lesson down so the horse can understand it, nor have they been consistent in the lesson. Often, the problem is miscommunication between the person and horse and a lack of education on the person's part. Many people lack the teaching skills needed to work with a "student." They need a lesson plan, and the better your lesson plan is, the more successful the outcome.

THE RIGHT WAY TO ASK

Horses are extremely polite. They're just mirror images of the person handling them, and they will seek the same level. From the time it's a couple of days old, the horse already knows how to do sliding stops and lead changes and can spin and balance itself in many ways. You can see a baby in the pasture doing all kinds of maneuvers we want them to do as an upper level performance horse. But when we start working with them, they won't do those things until we learn how to ask them correctly.

The moment we learn how to ask, a horse will start doing those things he already knows how to do naturally. If we don't learn how to ask until the horse is twenty years old, he will wait until then to start doing that maneuver. If we fumble around, kick when we shouldn't kick, pull when we shouldn't pull, and lean when we shouldn't lean, the horse will simply wait on us until we figure it out.

Once you find the very best ways to ask horses to do things, the variance in the way you ask different horses is very small. All horses are "straight A" students. They have a ninety percent retention rate over an eighteen-month period, and there are horses that will even do better than that.

Of course, there are horses that really don't want to learn. They would rather do their own thing, so they argue and fight every step of the way. At the other extreme, some horses become very frustrated because they want to learn but they don't understand what you want. Many times, a horse that seems difficult and slow to learn at first will do pretty well once he catches on.

REMARKABLE ADAPTABILITY

It's physically impossible for a horse to be stubborn, and yet they are accused of it all the time. If you consider how adaptable horses are, it's really quite remarkable. They adapt themselves to live both in some of the hottest and coldest places on earth. Mustangs, for example, can live on millions of acres, take care of all their own needs, and live a pretty long life.

But horses can also adapt and live in a five-by-ten-foot stall and have all of their needs taken care of. They adapt and go over jumps; they adapt and chase cattle; they do silly things like spin and run barrels. They rodeo and carry policemen through traffic in New York City. They adapt to pulling plows and wagons. And when I am training and I try to explain something to them, they adapt to my style.

So you really have to say that horses are adaptable. When you look up the meaning of adaptable, it means flexible and changeable, which is the opposite of stubborn. Stubborn means demanding, rigid, and unchangeable—not a good definition of the horse. Someone can hit a horse in the head every day for twenty years, but I can come along and work with them and, in a couple of hours, they won't be head-shy anymore. In that case, what happened is that the horse quickly adapted to a new environment.

When people say a horse is stubborn, they are really looking in the mirror; stubborn often does fit people as a description. We have this romantic idea that we're fitting into the horse's world but he is really fitting into ours. He's the one making all the changes while we make all the demands. In most cases, people aren't willing to put in the time or effort to learn how to teach the horse. If they don't want to make that effort, who is being stubborn?

The horse is a social animal. God made him that way. He likes company and he likes structure. If horses can't have the company of other horses, they'll take our company instead. But are we really doing them a favor? When we take a horse out on a trail ride, we are going to put a fifty-pound saddle on his back while he carries us around for four hours and gets hot and sweaty. He may see all kinds of things that scare the heck out of him. We'll be going on and over things that will make him worry about losing his footing. He may worry about losing his friends and worry about getting back to the barn in time to eat. If the horse could, he might say, "I'd rather pass on that." Wouldn't you? The point is that you can't really sell the idea that we're fitting into the horse's world.

BREEDING AND APTITUDE

You can tell a champion through his ability and his attitude toward wanting to learn. Often, the horses that really stand out are a little more difficult to work with, but they bring that difficulty as presence into the show ring as a kind of positive tension; they come out looking like a big ball of muscle and they just glow. In the ring, these horses look as if they're putting 110 percent into everything they do. Their attitudes and their work ethics make them outstanding. Many horses that have this extra drive can be challenging to work with. On the other hand, some world champions are simply sweet, good-natured horses that are calm and easygoing.

Some people also have a natural aptitude while others take much longer to learn. Nonetheless, people with less aptitude can still get along with their horses and enjoy them. It is also true with both people and horses that some have the ability and talent but not the desire and work ethic.

Breeding can come into play as well. What I have found is that, if you work with a horse that is above average or exceptional, he's going to have above-average papers. And, as a rule, if you buy a great horse, he's going to have great papers. But breeding isn't a guarantee. A horse can have above-average papers and still be average to poor. This is true for all breeds. The truth is, there are bigger differences within breeds than there are between breeds.

Each breed has its inborn advantages. I've had Appaloosas, palominos, Quarter Horses, Tennessee Walkers, Arabians, and Clydesdales. I have the most well-known Appaloosa in

the world: Bright Zip. Some people carry a prejudice against some of these breeds. Generally, they are not speaking through firsthand knowledge but are simply regurgitating what they've heard other people say. You can liken it to automobiles. There are cars to take vacations in and there are dump trucks to haul dirt with. If you try to haul dirt in a

convertible, it doesn't work too well; but it doesn't mean a convertible is useless. It is the same way with different breeds of horses.

Each individual breed also has its own special qualities. We don't try to make mules into Quarter Horses, but you can take that animal and enhance what that breed does well. Mules are quicker to learn things, so we're more careful not to let them learn habits we don't want them to have. For example, if a horse has been dragging a person off with a lead rope for years, I can fix that in a few hours. If a mule has dragged a person off with a lead rope three times, it might

take me a month to get it out of the mule's mind. That's why I am careful to not let a mule learn something that might be considered a bad habit.

For my personal use, I prefer horses that are easy-going and really like to learn. I no longer have to prove anything to anyone or to myself, which means that I don't have to take the really difficult horses and fix them. I get those every day in my work. Instead, I want a nice gelding that, if I leave him alone for six months, he's the same when I come back—like I just climbed off of him yesterday.

A New Insight

I've been giving clinics and seminars full-time since 1980. A couple of years ago, I learned what it is that horses really want, and that insight completely changed the way I've been handling horses for twenty-five years. What they want is the same thing people want, and that is peace.

When you think about it, what people really want more than anything else is peace—more than they want a big bank account or even companionship. Horses want exactly the same thing. Using that principle, I realized I don't have to

You have to find motivators for horses just like you have to find motivators for people. Most people don't work very well in a negative environment, and neither do horses. You can focus on telling people what they're doing wrong but it's more effective to focus on what you want them to do right. With people, sometimes you have to let them hunt around and find the answers themselves, and in many cases, you must do the same thing with horses.

Horses teach us to become better people and better teachers of other people. They teach us the importance of leaving our emotions out of the training. You can't get on a horse while thinking about other things in your life. You can't get on a horse mad. When training, you are trying to get the horse to become a mirror image of yourself. If you want the horse to change his behavior, you have to change your behavior first. These are principles you can test, and they work equally well when you are dealing with other people.

Horses know within a few minutes how much the person riding them knows. If the horse knows more than the person and figures out that he can do what he wants, a lot of times, he will. If you put someone who doesn't know the maneuvers on a world champion reining horse, in ten minutes, that horse will look like it couldn't win anything. Put someone who doesn't know anything on a world-class dressage horse, and that horse will look like a runaway.

make a horse stop kicking. He doesn't really want to kick. I don't have to make him stop throwing his head; he doesn't want to throw his head. I don't have to make him stop spooking or being nervous because he doesn't want that either. All I have to do is show him that there is a place he can relax and be at peace. I can show him that when he has his head in this particular spot, the whole world is better. I don't ever have to correct or scold. I just need to show him that spot where he can relax. When you watch this, it's almost magical. Horses respond to it rapidly—often within minutes. It has completely changed how I approach the horse.

In general though, horses have a good disposition. God made them that way. That's why so many people own horses. They don't own zebras and they don't own tigers. Horses are God's favorite animal. He gave them their strength and their beauty. God likes forgiveness, so He put forgiveness in the horse. The horse, as we acknowledge our past mistakes with him and we make a change, will not hold the past against us.

As a boy, Leon Harrel worked alongside his father and grandfather who farmed and raised cattle in Oklahoma.
Early on, these men instilled in Leon the western way of life and the hard work it took to maintain it. As he grew,
Leon began to dream of one day becoming a World Champion cowboy. After growing up and moving
to California, he became involved in rodeo. Bull riding was his passion until 1962 when a near-fatal spill
left him unable to continue in the sport.

Leon then began training race horses for G.D. Turnbull, but he missed the western element he loved so much.
Then in 1968, Leon discovered the grace and beauty of the cutting horse. Their strength, stamina, and cunning
challenged Leon and fueled his dreams. He began to concentrate fully on the cutting horse business in 1969,
and in 1972, he purchased his first training facility.

Leon has realized his childhood dream of becoming a World Champion cowboy five times over. He has claimed
the NCHA Futurity Championship twice, and has qualified for the finals twenty-three times in twenty-eight years.
Not only is Leon one of the most consistent winners in major cutting horse competition, he is widely recognized
by other horsemen as one of the world's leading cutting horse trainers. He is also a former President of the NCHA,
and was inducted into the NCHA Hall of Fame in 1989.

THE HORSE AND DOG MAN

Leon Harrel

I grew up in Oklahoma with ranchers and farmers and was riding way before I can remember. I always loved horses and dogs when I was a kid. The big joke among my family members was calling me "the horse and dog man." I've always had a tremendous love for the horse and I'd do anything to get on horseback.

In 1964, I went to work for G.D. Turnbull, whose primary source of income was training Quarter Horses for racing. Sonny Fields, who was running Turnbull Enterprises, had been heavily involved in performance horses and was an excellent cutting horse trainer. We'd ride race horses in the morning and cut cattle in the afternoon. The cutting took ahold of me, and I've never looked back since. It's been my life.

I've specialized in cutting horses since 1968. It's a wonderful game because of the mental contact necessary between the rider and horse. My greatest advantage was the opportunity to be with all of the major players who made up the cornerstone of the cutting industry when I was coming along: people like Buster Welch, Shodie Friedman, and the Bush family.

I was lucky enough that, while traveling through the country to different shows, I could go to their ranches and work with these top cutting horse people. There were very few people who would teach at that time. These men weren't teachers and they didn't want to share much—except for Buster, who was a great communicator. But by going to the ranches, working with them on a daily basis, and becoming friends

with them, they shared a lot of things with me that they normally didn't put out. I was very fortunate.

One of the things I learned was that you can't train a great champion through fear. It has to be done through trust, confidence, and consistency; by showing the horse how easy it is and not how hard. Keep it simple and show him in stages. If you showed a child how hard the fourth grade is when he was in the first grade, he wouldn't come back anymore. Teach a horse how to play this game in increments as the time allows. If you build a horse's confidence, he'll give you everything he has and more when you really need him. He'll throw his heart over the barn for you, and his body will follow.

When there is undue pressure to win, people often rush the process. You can destroy a horse this way because they don't think they're ever going to please you anyway. Pretty soon, the horse draws a blank and then, bingo! You're afoot. People, too, must be trained in stages. They may talk about wanting to compete and someday go to the national futurity, but if you told them how tough it was to win and how the odds are against them, they'd go buy a boat. Build them one brick at a time, and by golly, you might just end up with a winner.

WINNING

One of my most successful students was Todd Bemat, who has placed in the futurities several times and won just about everything there is to win. He worked for me a couple of summers when he was in high school and for two or three years when he got out. He is a natural talent and has a great love for horses. He is great with people too—a nice person and an extraordinary horseman.

I don't think the thrill of winning ever wears off, and I can remember each win like it was yesterday. I've won the futurity twice, and won just about every major contest there is. My first world championship was the NCHA Futurity Championship of 1974. It was an extraordinary feeling. The feeling made me wilder than a bull in a china closet, but you have to have the right attitude about winning.

When you lose, there are no excuses, and when you win, there are no apologies. That's the best way to handle it. If you've had a win like that, it's important to stay humble. You can enjoy your victories as much as anyone would, but everyone knows you won. You don't have to make a fool out of yourself by becoming a pompous cowboy who no one else can stand to be around. Instead, you should hold yourself up to that title and be a true champion by setting an example in the sport.

The pressure many champions put on themselves is thinking that every time they compete, they have to be the winner. The more they push this issue, the less they win. You might believe that everyone is expecting you to win, but people really don't care; they are concerned about their own wins. More important is to be someone other people can look up to and not be afraid to be around just because you're a world champion.

The last time I won the futurity, I was especially thrilled because there were a lot of circumstances involved. For one thing, the horse I won on, Smart Days, was of the first crop of Smart Little Lenas. And the man who started her, Shodie Friedman, was a dear friend of mine who had become very ill with emphysema. He was there and held herd for me. Then I drew terribly in the finals, but somehow, it just happened. All the circumstances around that win made it very special.

I've had a lot of really nice horses, but probably the most fun mare was Doc's Playmate. She was extraordinary. She would give you one hundred percent every time you asked her. Conditions made no difference to her, whether the arena was terribly deep or hard, the cattle were good or bad, or whether you'd hauled her two days and nights straight through—she didn't care. She was just a winner. The better care you took of her, the better care she took of you. The funny part is she wasn't really a people lover. She just loved winning; loved having her picture taken.

To be a winner takes the right attitude combined with consistency in your training. Do what it takes to win, but do those things in a timely fashion and in a non-violent way. There is no room for extreme training procedures. Horses are like children and need the same kind of guidance. When they're good, they need to know they were good, and when it comes time for correction, do it in a way they can understand. If you're mad, get off the horse and go get a drink of water. Go to the house. Just get away from him. You are not going to teach a horse anything when you're mad.

52

I'm probably learning more about people and horses than I ever did because of the Galles Harrel clinics we are teaching. We have people coming from all over the world. In the teaching field, the first thing you should understand is that there are people who really want to compete; people who kind of want to compete; and people who are just doing it for fun. You must treat them accordingly. The people who are just doing it for fun don't want to be Buster Welch, so you can't have the same expectations of them.

What I'm learning about horses through these clinics is how very tolerant they are of the human being! This is especially true with the cutting horse. These horses love this game so much that they will put up with the nearly impossible on a daily basis, and still want to play with a cow. It's a lot of fun for everyone.

Young trainers should understand that, just because a horse isn't bred to the ultimate on both sides, if someone wants the horse trained, they should give it the proper attention. He may not know how he's bred; he may just want to be a winner. I won a futurity on Doc's Playmate, who was out of an old mare that had only produced roping horses. I rode this mare and she was so cowwy that when she saw a cow, she'd just go to pieces. It was because of the mother that I bought Doc's Playmate as a two-year-old. She was a winner who made it to the NCHA Horses Hall of Fame.

An awakening had come for me earlier when I bought Fizzabar, another Hall of Fame horse, from Don Dodge in 1970. Until I rode that mare, I never really knew what I was searching for. It was then I knew what it was supposed to feel like. Once you know the feel, you're no longer just searching. The fun part about working with these great horses is that, although you'll never have another one like them, there will be little things about them that you will be reminded of in other horses. If you can piece that together with the individual you are training, then you're in business.

I'm spending most of my time putting on cutting clinics now, and I'm no longer riding twenty-five horses a day. It's a whole different kind of fun. I'm at a point now where I can really give back to the sport that has allowed me to meet people from all over the world and to be whatever I wanted to be. You talk about lucky!

I'm as excited about this industry now as when I first discovered it. In fact, I wake up sometimes and want to pinch myself. You can change people's lives with cutting horses, the same way they changed mine. We might work with a lady whose husband has died, and maybe she was a timid person to start with. With this sport, she can have a new focus in life, and we can help build her up. It's hard to believe how it can change people's lives.

THE HORSE

Man has always had a natural affinity for the horse. If a person can become a silent partner, guiding them, developing them, and caring for them, the two can develop a stronger bond than most people realize. You can become someone they want to hang out with. Horses want a leader, and you can be that leader.

I like to develop horses with what I call the TASTE method, which stands for Trust, Accountability, Support, Truth, and Energy. These are the same things you would offer a family member or good friend. Trust means that you trust that they're going to give you everything they have to give you. And trust is a two-way street. With your consistency and the way you've dealt with them, when you ask them to do something different, they're going to trust you also.

Accountability is a commitment that you will be consistent. And support means that when they've done what you've asked them to do, you let them know they've done well. You can correct a horse and still remain its friend. Some cowboys have a thing about not ever petting them or showing affection, but I love to pet a horse.

Truth means teaching horses things that are true to the sport they are going to be performing in. Energy refers to your demeanor around the horse, which should be kind, positive, and upbeat. People think a horse doesn't know how you feel, but they do know. That is why horses and dogs will approach some people and don't want to have anything to do with others. It's the energy they feel around certain people.

Probably eighty percent of the people who attend our training schools are women. Women didn't get too involved in cutting in the past, although there were a few in the non-pro sector who were double-tough. Because of women's sensitivity, their connection with the horse is often stronger than men's. If a woman knows what she is trying to accomplish with a horse, she can do as well as or better than a man. This is why women are now dominating the amateur and non-pro classes.

One reason the western scene has become so popular for both men and women is because of the times we are now going through. Life is going at such a fast pace, and there is much violence in the world. On top of that, both parents are having to work and kids are growing up too fast. People are looking for a slower and a simpler time, and what do we have to look back to? We look back to our western heritage. For the most part, that's not the cowboy; it's the horse that symbolizes that heritage.

We have all the literature in the world about the horse available today. We have gurus teaching people how to handle horses. Most trainers who are respected today use non-violent methods, so the message they're getting out to the public is non-violence. This is a great thing.

If someone wants to get into a discipline, there are all kinds of books and videos. John Lyons and I did the first cutting video in 1982, and now there are many good videos. This means a person doesn't have to go through a long trial and error period to make things work for them.

At the same time, people involved with horses are getting the kind of quality time that helps slow their worlds down and improve their lives. Being involved with cutting horses has certainly improved mine.

One thing I'd like to do before I die is to win the futurity one more time. If it's supposed to happen, it will happen; but I don't go out every year putting undue pressure on myself because of my past accomplishments or make myself miserable if I don't win. Like your birthday—they can't take those wins away from you. Hold onto your victories and treasure them, but go on with your life, and have a big time!

Known among his peers in the horse industry as the "King of Stock Horses," Ronnie Richards has had a winning career both as a competitor and a world-class trainer. Ronnie started his own horse training business in Irvine, California, in 1955 at age eighteen. On Lucky Libra, he won California's richest stock horse event in 1961. His many other titles include the 1966 Santa Barbara Nationals championship and the Cow Palace Mare Class in 1972.

On the unregistered mare, Mona Lisa, Ronnie impressed the entire industry with his spectacular wins. Other winners he trained include talented horses such as Scooter Reigh, Hackamore Stakes Champion Ebony Chex, and Cow Palace Champion Poppa Chex. Ronnie won Santa Barbara Championship and Reserve titles on Cheshire Chex and Moon Chex, the Bakersfield Cow Horse Classic on Lucky Mac, and the Cow Palace on King Jay Bar.

On other great horses such as Who Knows and Speedy Cash, Ronnie won in the Open "A" Stock Horse Division more times than any other competitor. He is credited with turning out more International and American Horse Show Association Medal Finalists than any other trainer. In addition, he qualified seventeen horses for the NRCHA World Championship Snaffle Bit Futurity Finals and was reserve champion on Me O' Lena in 1981. Ronnie has served as an AHSA, AQHA, and NRCHA judge and as NRCHA Director of Judges, and he was named the National Reined Cow Horse Association Stock Horseman of the Year in 1997.

THE TRAITS OF A GENUINE HORSEMAN

Ronnie Richards

My father wasn't a professional trainer, but he was as great a horseman as ever lived. I taught strictly reined cow horses and cutting horses before I retired, but earlier in my career, I taught children in every phase of western horse training. I had my own stables and started training when I was eighteen, training kids to compete in the American Horse Show Association Medal Finals, which was held once a year. It was a big event in those years, and I was fortunate enough to train the most winners in that event. I also trained for the International Stock Seat Finals and trained open horses—pleasure, trail, and stock horses. I had the ability to teach children and I was very successful at it.

I've had a successful career as a trainer but on my gravestone, I hope they write, "He was a great horseman." To me that's the ultimate—not to be just a horse trainer, but a horseman. A horseman knows how to care for a horse; how and what to feed, when to have the horse's teeth floated, when to have its feet done, what the right bedding is, and if and why it is sick. This is a type of knowledge we are quickly losing today.

Care. That's a big word. I learned about care from my dad, who was a true horseman. As a kid, I remember coming home and having a horse with bandages on his legs I needed to take care of. If I had a date, I might bandage him up

quickly after riding so I could hurry to leave for my date. I remember coming home and checking on my horse, and finding bandages lying in the middle of the aisle. I knew my dad had checked, and maybe he found a wrinkle in the bandage or something else that just wasn't right. I didn't have to ask—I knew I was to do it again.

From that, I learned that there is a reason for all the things we do to care for a horse. My dad absolutely would not tolerate careless treatment of a horse. There are thousands of horse trainers today, but many of them are not horsemen. They've never taken the time to learn how to take care of a horse properly, so if something goes wrong and they can't get to a vet, that horse may die. Some people see a horse as a vehicle for them to win with, and they have no real love for that horse. Those are people I have no respect for because of the way I was taught.

WAITING FOR NITA

When I was nine years old, my dad and I went to a horse sale where I saw a two-year-old Thoroughbred and Standard Bred mare. She was called Nita. There was something about her that just made me fall in love with her. I wanted my dad to buy her, but we were poor folks. He bid on her and went as far as he could, but she sold for $800 or $900—more than we could afford. Still, I kept track of her over the years. Eventually, she was sold to a fella who started racing her in stake races. Pretty soon, she became sillier than a hoot owl!

I was twelve years old by then, and I had a mare I was showing and winning on. The man who owned Nita had a young son he wanted to buy a horse for. He heard I had always liked this mare, and he called to ask me to trade. My dad had seen how silly the mare had gotten and didn't want me to trade. All of our trainer friends advised me against it, saying, "You don't want that silly son-of-a-gun!" Finally, my dad told me we could only afford for me to keep one horse, and if I traded and she didn't get any better—well, then that's what I would have.

Against everyone's advice, I made the trade. I had wanted her when she was a baby and couldn't have her, and when I finally got her, she was an older horse and was crazy. I worked Nita for six months before I showed her. I won that first show, and then won forty-six classes in a row on her. She was never defeated. As a kid, she was my pet, and I kept her until she died.

When you buy a good gelding and their show career is over, they're done. But when you buy a good mare, you can breed her and keep the lineage going. Nita was not registered, but my daughter just won the Snaffle Bit Futurity on Nita's granddaughter.

Through the years, I bought a lot of horses off the ranch that looked to me like they had the ability to make show horses, although many weren't registered. One such horse I trained and showed was Mona Lisa, who was probably the greatest reined cow horse that ever lived—and that's not just my opinion; it is shared by many. Mona Lisa was out of a ranch mare by a Thoroughbred stud. She was an outstanding mare—a beautiful chestnut with a big white face and two white hind socks. In 1963, I bought her for a customer from Don Dodge. Don had done a lot with her but she had started going down hill. I was able to bring her back, and she won for five more years. What set Mona Lisa apart was her athletic ability and her attitude.

I had another little horse I bought after I saw a ranch cowboy riding him in a junior show. He was a very ugly little horse—bad confirmation, big head, thick neck. But I saw something

in him I liked. I bought him for a little bit of nothing, took him home, and told my wife, "I bought you a horse." When I unloaded him out of the trailer, she said, "If you think I'm riding that ugly son-of-a-gun, you're crazy!" I worked him for about a month, and she finally came out one day and watched me spinning and stopping him. With a big smile, she said, "Boy, my horse is working good, isn't he?"

She rode him from then on, and he won every bridle horse stake in California. We called him "Who Knows" because people would ask, "How's the ugly little horse working?" and I'd reply, "Who knows?" They used to make fun of him, but

he sure turned pretty when he was having his picture taken with his blue ribbons! This happened throughout the years. I would see horses I felt had something special, and I would work with them awhile to bring out their talents. They often turned out to be great.

But the business is different today. The big horse shows now have big prizes, and money has become more important. Consequently, there are a lot of horses that have probably been passed over because they didn't make it right off the bat. With the big prizes that can be won in the three-year-old classes, they have to be good right away. If a horse

doesn't show talent immediately, many trainers will simply get another one.

We showed mainly in the open shows like Del Mar in California, the Cow Palace in San Francisco, and the California State Fair. In these big open events, which lasted ten to twelve days, the western horses, gaited horses, and hunter/jumpers all showed together. These events are no more, and neither is the fun in many ways. Today, you go there to compete, and you'd better have a tough one!

TRAINING SUCCESS

Our family has always been in the horse business and will be for years to come. I quit training professionally at fifty-six, but my daughters are both married to horse trainers whose fathers are in the Horse Trainers Hall of Fame. Laurie is married to John Ward, and Susie is married to John Rosier. They are two of the most outstanding trainers of reined cowhorses in the country.

To me, the Quarter Horse is the easiest to train and the best athlete. They're very versatile, and they have the mind to be able to do anything you ask them to do. Their cow sense and ability to work a cow are far superior to any other horse. I train every horse as an individual and have never had a set pattern every horse had to work. I try to figure out a horse's mental state and what I feel he can accept. The horse will tell you if you're going too fast or pushing too hard, and pushing too hard can make a good horse into a rattlebrain. I've had the ability to communicate well enough with a horse to know how far I can go with him.

I also believe if you're kind to horses, they will try harder. A few horses that are winning today have a mortal fear of their riders. A horse can only last so long like that and eventually, he won't take it anymore. He will either panic or quit completely. These tactics can produce winners in the short run, and once the horse is ruined, it's easy enough for trainers to get another horse. But to me, a great horse trainer is one who can keep a horse and win on him for five or six years.

I took a lot of pride in that many of my horses weren't overnight successes, but they lasted for years and years in the show ring. Years ago, I saw a mare called Lucky Libra. She was a great reining horse but the man who owned her was putting too much pressure on her. I asked him to turn her out for six months, and I would come back and buy her. After I had worked with her, a man wanted to buy her. I said yes, with the stipulation that he give me one year to work with her without showing. He agreed to those terms and paid a lot of money for her. When Lucky Libra came back into the show ring after her time off, she won almost every class I ever showed her in. She showed for about eight years, and was one of the greatest.

THE THRILL OF WINNING

The first year I won on Mona Lisa at the Cow Palace, which was the biggest reined cowhorse event at the time, the cast of *Bonanza* was there and the place was packed. I worked a cow on that mare and she was so great that, when I went out to get the trophy and saddle, all of those thousands of people stood up and applauded and continued applauding until we were all the way out to the pen. Many of those people had no idea what was happening out there; they could only tell from all of the excitement that she was the best. When I went back to the stall area, they had to bring ushers in because so many people had come out of the stands to see that magnificent horse. I'll never forget that thrill.

Watching other riders succeed is equally thrilling. I was once judging a junior show, and there was a little girl who entered every class throughout the day. She had a beat-up old saddle and bridle that weren't in the popular style of the time. Her horse wasn't very pretty, but he was groomed to perfection, and she was as neat as a pin. You could see there had been a lot of care taken on this horse, but he was way out of his class because the best horses were there.

I couldn't place her, but every time I looked at her I'd think, "Gosh, look how hard that little ol' gal is trying. There is no more drive than in that little girl." As the day went on, I wished more and more that I could place her, but I had top people in those classes. Then came the bareback equitation class, and here comes this little girl. I could see that she'd probably ridden bareback most of her life because she couldn't get the saddle on by herself. Someone had taught her how to have a good seat, and this little girl never moved a muscle.

I had a lot of tough competitors in that class, but I ended up bringing her and one other rider back into the ring, and I asked them to mount and dismount. The other rider, a bigger girl, rode a horse that was only about 14.2, but she struggled to get on. But the other girl, who had a pretty tall horse, grabbed the mane and swung up there like it was nothing. I was happy to give her first place.

Every year, they gave a big memorial trophy at this show and it happened that in this year, it was given for the bareback

equitation class. After the show, I passed by an old Buick with an old trailer and sitting on the hood was this big trophy. It made me smile, and when I did, the little girl stopped me. "Can I kiss you, Mr. Richards?" she asked. That was the biggest thrill I ever got judging a horse show!

MEASURING ACCOMPLISHMENT

When you find a horse you think will make it, spend a year getting him ready, and then compete in the big event where he comes through for you, it's a thrilling achievement. It's a thrill also to work with a green rider who didn't ride very well and bring them along to the point where they win a big championship. My feeling of accomplishment is that I've been able to succeed in this business and find that my peers regard me as one of the best there has been. I know my family is going to say that, but when my peers say it, it really feels great.

When you are showing, you're only as good as the horse you're sitting on. And if you don't win, pretty soon you'll be going by the wayside. You have to win to be considered in the top echelon and if you're not in that category, you won't make it in this business. Consequently, if you don't have a good horse you can win on, you had better break one yourself or find a good one somewhere.

Finding a good horse is both an instinct and something you learn along the way. I was a champion because I had good horses and had the ability to train them to win, and that's what it's all about. That said, I have also learned to listen to other people's opinions. I don't feel I'm to the point of being so stubborn that I can't learn something new. It's what you learn after you know it all that counts.

th them awhile to bring out their talents. They often turned out to be great.

versatile, and they have the mind to be able to do anything you ask them to do.

Bob Avila, of Temecula, California, is often referred to as "the trainer's trainer."
He is also described as one of the most versatile and accomplished horsemen of the last thirty-five years.
Accumulating over thirty-seven world champion and reserve titles during his career, Bob has performed in events
ranging from performance to halter. He received the first AQHA Professional Horseman Award
and is one of only two horsemen to have won both the $100,000 NRCHA Futurity
and the $100,000 NRHA Futurity.

Bob won the title of World's Greatest Horseman in 2000, and in the last few years,
he has taken home five Stallion Stakes Futurity championships, three Snaffle Bit Futurity championships,
and one NRHA Futurity Championship. These wins have helped him achieve career earnings
of over $1.5 million between the NRHA and the NRCHA.

FINDING YOUR WAY

Bob Avila

I was born into a horse family. My dad competed in rodeos and both my parents showed horses. In fact, my father is still a horse trainer. With my parents' influence, I started showing horses when I was five; but like many kids, I went through a time of rebellion as a teenager. When I was sixteen, I quit riding horses and let my hair grow. My interests switched to driving fast cars and chasing women! This type of rebellion, I think, is typical of many kids that age.

After high school, I moved to Reno and dabbled with college, but it didn't hold my interest. I ended up with a very good job working for Goodyear Tire Company, and I was there for three years. Still, I had a sense that something wasn't right. When I was almost twenty-one, I was driving to work one day when suddenly it came to me that working with horses was what I really wanted to do. I suppose I had never really gotten that out of my blood.

Now the question was where to go to work. I could have gone back to work with my dad but I didn't at that time; every kid knows more than his father for a period in his life, and that was mine. Instead, I called Tony Amarel, Sr., who was one of my idols in the horse world when I was a kid. I was lucky because Tony had a spot for me. I first called him on a Saturday, and I was working with him the next Monday morning.

On Tony's ranch, I did every job imaginable. You name it, I did it. I cleaned stalls, rode horses, fed horses and cattle, and built fences. If you're going to do this job, you just have to accept the fact that there is a lot of work to do on a ranch. After a few years, I finally did go back to work with my father. At the time, he had a horse named Doc's Dee Bar, who is now listed in the new *Western Horse Legends* book. After working with my father awhile, I went out on my own as a trainer.

You don't realize how much you've learned from other people until you are out on your own and have to rely on yourself to produce. I found myself sitting at night reflecting on what went on that day, and I would remember how I'd seen certain things handled in the past. Then I would go back the next day and try those same things, and it was at those times I could appreciate how much I had learned in the past. But at the end of the day, I had to take what my father and everyone else had taught me and learn to make it work for me.

HORSEMANSHIP FUNDAMENTALS

If you're going to be successful in the horse industry, you must love what you are doing and you must love your animals. If you use your animals only as a means to an end, you may win, but you'll never be successful in the long run. You have to have a feeling for your horses.

When a person sees a horse only as a tool, they don't always do what's best for the animal. People often try to force horses into doing things they will rebel against, and when the horse does rebel, they take it out on the horse. People sometimes ask me how to get their horses to do something they want them to do, and I often have to tell them that maybe their horse just isn't cut out to do that. It's the same way that I'm not cut out to be a surgeon, for example. Instead of trying to force them to do things they don't excel at, you must find what a particular horse is good at doing, and then encourage them to do it as well as they can. When you are forcing behavior rather than teaching new skills, most horses will look for an out. Sooner or later, they will rebel.

In the past, we thought of "breaking" horses, but today people think more about training. Today there are many clinics, books, DVDs, and horse programs on television. Much more education is available for young people getting involved with horses. Of course, there is also a lot of excellent marketing going on, and we need to be selective about whose methods we choose to follow.

In my experience, training horses is somewhat like training three-year-old children. Lessons must be repeated over and over again for a three-year-old to learn something new. You may have to keep repeating, "No, don't touch that," and sometimes, you have to slap their hands. You have to require both children and horses to pay attention to you and mind you, but at the same time, you must teach them how to do the right thing. It's important to remember that a horse is a creature of habit, and they can learn both good and bad habits.

The biggest secret in horse training is knowing when to quit. You can't continue to drum away at horses just because you are in a hurry for them to learn. If they do well, reward them and say, "That's enough for now. Let's go walk around." Staying at them is like keeping a kid in school all day with no recess. As often as possible, try to stop on a good note.

You can tell how much talent a horse has early in its training, but you can't always tell how much want it has. People are the same way. How many talented, intelligent people have you seen in your life who were lazy? They are missing the kind of drive it takes to be successful. I can relate horse behavior to people behavior in other ways as well. When I get stumped with a horse, I think of how I would handle a person in the same situation.

THE RIGHT MATCH

Matching a horse with its natural likes and abilities will always produce the best results. I showed a stud named Check's In My Pocket, a son of Doc O' Lena and King Fritz. He was bred royally, but he didn't like reining as a cow horse. He had so much talent that he would do it anyway, but he didn't enjoy it.

I explained that to the people who owned him, and said that I wanted to rope on him. The owners didn't want to own a roping horse and they sold him, but this horse loved roping. He was happy and fun to be around once he was allowed to do the thing he enjoyed. Check's In My Pocket ended up a world champion roping horse.

People also have their own likes when it comes to horses. I get along with horses that are a little quirky, but I don't enjoy horses you have to force into doing things—and they don't turn out to be the best show horses. Although you don't see it much anymore, we showed all-around horses when I was a kid. I work mostly with cow horses and reining now, but I've shown cutting horses, pleasure horses, halter horses, and roping horses. I've run barrels and I've shown English horses.

My mother used to say that my favorite event was the gate opening! But for many people—and horses too—there are

particular events they like most and can excel at, and there are types of horses they get along with best. For this and other reasons, I try not to mismatch a rider and a horse.

The key to success in this or any other industry is that you have to love what you're doing, believe in yourself, and believe in your product. It happens that the horses I train are my product and I always want to do my best. To be successful at anything—whether you're a horseman, a farmer, a doctor, or own a tire store—you have to love it, eat and breathe it, and not be afraid to get up in the morning and run at it every single day.

ver be successful in the long run. You have to have a feeling for your horses.

ew skills, most horses will look for an out. Sooner or later, they will rebel.

A seven-time World Champion team roper, Jake Barnes has been an inspiration to rodeo fans and athletes in all sports. His world titles in 1985-89, 1992, and 1994, as well as his other winnings, have brought career earnings approaching two million dollars.

During the fifth performance of the 2005 Wrangler National Finals Rodeo, Jake suffered a right thumb amputation that forced him out of the competition. Through his faith, hard work, and the support of the rodeo world, he thankfully has recovered and is back on the road doing what he loves best. In 2006, Jake won the average title at the Puyallup Pro Rodeo in Washington, and the Eastern Oregon Livestock Show & Rodeo in Union, Oregon. Born in Huntsville, Texas, Jake now lives in Scottsdale, Arizona, with his wife, Toni. The couple has three sons, Tuff, Bo Jake, and Anthony and two daughters, Sunny and Shelly.

In December 2006, Jake was honored at the Wrangler National Finals Rodeo Weekend in Las Vegas when he received an esteemed award at the Legends of ProRodeo Breakfast. He was selected to receive the Legends of ProRodeo Award, which honors exemplary character and leadership in the home, the arena, and the community.

THOUGHTS ON THE RODEO LIFE

Jake Barnes

My grandparents on both sides of my family were ranchers in eastern New Mexico, and I grew up around horses and cattle. My great-uncle, Jake McClure, was a world champion calf roper in the 1950s, and my father was an amateur roper. I went through the ranks from junior rodeo, to high school and college rodeo, to amateur rodeo. The first highlight in my career was making the National Finals in 1980.

I started halfway in the season, so it was very exciting. I wasn't sure how much talent I had, but it's every roper's dream to make it to the National Finals. I was twenty-one and knew nothing about the industry. Although I was thrown in the frying pan and didn't really know what I was doing, I had a really good partner, Allen Bach, who helped me through it.

What got me there more than anything else was determination. I just didn't want to fail. Rodeo was something I really wanted—the freedom of traveling around the country doing what I love, and making at least enough income to keep doing it. Out of about 7,800 PRCA members, maybe twenty-five percent make some kind of living at it. It's extremely hard to do that in rodeo because we pay our own entry fees and expenses.

THE RODEO GAME

PRCA competitors can enter seventy events each year. The costs of travel and horses has quadrupled since I began. This means you might make it to the national finals having spent $125,000, and you can win $78,000 there. Each year, the top guys win $150,000 to $200,000. This may seem like a lot of money, but after you take your expenses out of that, it's pretty slim pickin's. For rodeo to make any kind of financial sense, then, you have to be good enough to attract sponsorship. Today, rodeo is getting much more recognition and a lot more TV time than in the past, so we can attract the kind of sponsorship that can keep a cowboy afloat. The sponsors provide financial incentives for you to have a good year.

Anyone who has a great desire to rodeo should follow their dreams, but you have to be realistic. In many ways, it's a form of gambling. Only a small percentage will actually make a living at it, and it's a very tough way to earn an income. I'm fortunate to have lasted in the industry twenty-seven years and can say I've made a decent living at it. But I am also a seven-time world champion, so I've had a lot of perks along the way to keep me going. Even at this level, it's a tough way to support a family. What you earn from rodeo is based only on your performance, and sometimes there are lean years.

In addition to the pressures of earning a living, there are pitfalls in rodeo just as in all walks of life. One of these pitfalls is getting mixed up with alcohol or drugs, and there are other temptations of all kinds. I have been immature myself in the past and have made mistakes, but much of this can be avoided if you surround yourself with good people who won't deter you from what you're trying to accomplish.

One of the responsibilities that comes along with being a world champion is setting an example for the people who look up to you. When someone looks to me as a role model, I may have the opportunity to persuade them to take the right road. I tell them if they want to make it in the rodeo industry, these are the steps they should follow: Attend to business. Practice hard. And attract sponsorship.

To draw a sponsor, you can't have problems like getting drunk, using drugs, or getting into fights. No one is going to invest their time and money in you if you do. It's also just common sense that the people who are continually successful in life don't have those types of shortcomings. If you get involved in those things, somewhere along the line it will tear you down. Both in and out of the arena, I try to conduct myself as a role model kids can look up to.

WHEN THE GOING GETS TOUGH

Rodeo is a tough sport, but even though you compete against one another, the people involved in rodeo are really one big family. In 2005, I was in the middle of the National Finals Rodeo and in the driver's

seat to win my eighth championship when I had an accident. The stakes were high, and I gambled when I shouldn't have. The result was, I got my thumb caught in a rope and cut it off. I had to drop out of the finals, and it was a very emotional ordeal for me because I didn't think I was ever going to compete again. Of course, many ropers have lost thumbs, but no one before at this level.

I spent most of the following year rehabilitating and trying to get my confidence back, approaching it the way I approach everything else: with determination and hard work. I had to step it up mentally and work harder than ever. It was a difficult time, but now I'm back roping with my partner, Clay O'Brien Cooper.

After this accident, I got hundreds of calls from my competitors and from other people with great influence in the roping industry. I was amazed by all the calls and prayers. It was awfully lonely for a while because of the things going through my head. For twenty-six years, rodeo

had been a part of my life every day, and it was the way I'd always made a living. Suddenly, there was a chance I wouldn't be doing that anymore.

My faith in God and all of the encouragement people gave me allowed me to get through it. It was encouraging just hearing the other guys tell me that I would be back. I didn't always believe that at the time, but since they didn't seem to have any worries about me, I began to think, "Well, maybe I will be back." I am sometimes surprised that I've gotten back to this level, but at forty-seven, I feel my roping is as good as or better than it has ever been.

RODEO HORSES

When I grew up, the people around me generally thought of a horse as transportation. The deeper I got into my career, though, the more I figured out that being a better horseman increases the longevity of the horse. Before, I relied mostly on my ability and didn't use the horse's ability, but once you've had a great horse, you find out how much easier it makes your job.

I also learned that great horses come in all different packages. With the horse I won most of my championships on, he did his job and I did mine. Although he was extremely talented, I didn't really know what I had until he was done. At first I didn't realize his value because he didn't resemble the stereotype of a well-broke horse. He was tough, hard to manage, and wasn't really a fun horse to compete on. Although this horse had his quirks, he also had great athletic ability.

When his career was over and I couldn't replace him, it made me truly appreciate the value of having a great horse. A horse has to be physically and mentally tough in the rodeo industry, and he was so mentally tough that he was hard to manage. Like a racehorse, these horses have to have strength and speed but must also have the mind to keep those traits under control. We rely on the horse's speed and strength, but it must be contained. Competing so many days out of the year, we don't have the opportunity to train much so we try to buy horses we can win on right away.

Still, if I could start my career over, I would take some horsemanship classes. The techniques you learn could complement the roping industry. A horse won't be a success overnight, and I think some trainers are too harsh. If you're too aggressive, it hinders you.

I have to have a horse ready right now, and win on him right now. I pay premium dollar for the horses I buy, and I don't have the luxury of bringing them along slowly and hoping that if they're lacking experience in a certain area, it will come. But when you try to bring a horse up too quickly, it's a bad experience for them and can blow them up. If this happens, you will spend all your time trying to slow them back down.

THE RODEO LIFE

Cowboys go into rodeo because they like the lifestyle. It's certainly not the money—there's isn't anyone getting rich out here! I love the western lifestyle. I love horses; I love cattle. Even now, sometimes I'm out roping by myself and I say, "Man, I love roping!" It is all I ever wanted to do.

There has been a perception for years and years that rodeo cowboys are guys who like to get drunk and fight. Of course, there is still some of that out there, but when you're making a living, you don't have time for that. It is too demanding to keep up that pace while living the rodeo lifestyle. Some try to do that, but they don't survive in the industry.

I am certain that one purpose of the success I've had is to be able to be a mentor and pass along what I've learned to other inspired ropers. In fact, it doesn't matter if it's a roper; if anyone is taking the wrong path, I'm happy for the opportunity to be an influence in their life. I'm the first one to encourage someone to live a healthy life because I feel that we lose so many great talents through drugs and alcohol.

I believe you can get anything you want out of life with hard work and determination, but there are many stumbling blocks along the way. I could have been easily influenced at numerous points in my life, but thank God I was surrounded by the right types of role models.

I talk to young kids interested in rodeo through Christian groups, and I tell them what kinds of temptations they will

come up against, and that they will have to make a choice someday. I also tell them that everyone can't succeed at rodeo, and that they have to be prepared for the alternatives. In other words, they have to have a plan B. One way to prepare for that is to get a good education.

My priority is my faith in God, and I want to glorify Him in everything I do. My family is my second priority and I have to balance my work with their needs. I love the rodeo life, but if I go to too many events or put on too many roping clinics, my family life suffers. I have five children, ages thirteen to twenty-seven. My three boys have all roped and have been successful, but whether they choose to make a living at it is up to them. They have to find their own talents and the desires of their own hearts, and I plan to support them one hundred percent.

As for me, I'm getting toward the end of my career, but I'm going to be the very best I can until I recognize that my skills are starting to diminish to the point that I'm not competitive enough to be at the top. Today, I feel I'm roping better than ever, so I will cross that bridge when I get there. I've spent twenty-seven years going night and day, so when that time comes, I think I'll sit back and smell the roses. I'll watch my kids grow and, hopefully, teach them some of my skills. But for now, I work every day to improve my roping and my horsemanship.

The people you meet going up, you're going to meet again coming back down. You have to keep your composure and stay confident, but that is different than being arrogant. It's a double-edged sword that you have to be a very confident person to survive but still have to be humble. I don't use my success to try to get an edge. I'm just a person who loves what I do—in fact, I can't understand why everyone doesn't love it as much as I do! I believe that God gave me the talent, and I'm going to exercise it to the maximum while keeping in mind that there is a greater purpose for my success.

Before, I relied mostly on my ability and didn't use the horse's ability, but a

But when you try to bring a horse up too quickly, it's a bad experience for them

ce you've had a great horse, you find out how much easier it makes your job.

and you blow them up. If this happens, you will spend all your time trying

Ron Ralls was raised on a California cattle ranch in the rugged hill country between Tehachapi and Lake Isabella. He lived the life of a working cowboy until his late twenties, when some difficult ranching years and a chance meeting with celebrated trainer Monty Roberts of Flag Is Up Farms in Santa Ynez Valley sparked a new career for Ron in the working cow horse show world.

Highlights of Ron's many achievements include winning the 2003 and 2004 World's Greatest Horseman Contest on two different horses: Cowgirls Are Smart and A Chic 'N Time. His other wins include the Silver Legacy Reno Snaffle Bit Futurity on Captain Nice; the Florida Snaffle Bit Futurity in 2003 and 2004; the Georgia Snaffle Bit Futurity; the Ardmore Snaffle Bit Futurity; Reserve Reno Snaffle Bit Futurity 2003; the Salinas Bridle Class; and the Salinas Hackamore Class.

Ron showed in California before starting a training facility in Texas near Gainesville. Adding to his wins, he won the World's Richest Stock Horse Contest on A Chic 'N Time in 2006.

FROM THE RANCH TO THE SHOW ARENA

Ron Ralls

I grew up on a large cow and calf ranch in California and stayed there until I was twenty-eight years old. We had a family ranch, about fifty-thousand acres, that was very rough, steep, and brushy. It was easy to lose cows in this type of country, and the main thing my dad stressed was that if we were out gathering cows, everyone had better be where they were supposed to be and thinking right. One small mistake could cost you a whole day's work looking for lost cows.

It was important to my dad to ride a nice horse. He would always say, jokingly, that the only reason he had those cows around was so we would have something to work our horses on. Of course, that wasn't true—the cows were his living, but he did enjoy riding and making a nice horse. He produced some pretty nice ranch horses.

My dad had the notion that no matter what your horse did, you'd better get to the spot where you needed to get so you didn't lose those cows. I think the way I grew up on that ranch made a difference in the way I would later work cows in an arena. From the time we were kids, we worked all the time and were happy to do so. It was just part of the deal. My dad raised us with a strong work ethic, and I try to keep that every day.

THOUGHTS ON TRAINING

When I was in my late twenties, I got acquainted with Monty Roberts through my brother, who was a veterinarian. Monty showed stock horses and had a ranch. He sent a couple of young horses home with me to work with for six months. I don't know if

88

he was impressed with the work I did with those horses or thought it was so horrible he should help me, but he told me if I moved to his place in Solvang, California, he would set me up with a barn, get me customers, and help me get started in the horse show industry. I suppose he thought he saw some talent there somewhere. With drought affecting the ranch, I took him up on the offer. Monty and his wife, Pat, were very generous people.

I started showing horses in 1984. Many young guys out of college will go to work for a successful horse trainer, but I was twenty-eight when I started and didn't do that. Monty Roberts taught me many of the fundamentals of training a show horse. One thing I learned from him was to use reverse motion as a correction if a horse walks forward out of a turnaround. Most people walk them forward to help them get across and to learn. I do it the exact opposite.

Among the things my father taught me that still make sense to me today is that horses should keep their hind feet up under them at all times; they have to use their hocks and stop before they turn with a cow. That's something he always drilled into us, and it has remained a foundation of my training philosophy.

Unfortunately, some trainers just train for the show and they don't care about the horse beyond the futurity. That leads to cutting corners and asking a horse to be better than God designed him to be. It is like constantly stepping on the gas pedal—asking that horse for his life when there's no need to. I can't think that way. There is a life after the futurity for that horse. If you don't care about the future of a horse beyond his first show, you don't have much compassion for the animal. You might be better off being a racecar driver. You can put a new transmission or engine in a car and it won't be as big a deal as damaging a good horse.

I have my own ideas about what makes a good horse. If I am looking at a yearling that hasn't been started, for instance, I put him in a smaller round pen and just watch him move. I want to see a horse that doesn't really like to take his neck up past level. I would prefer to have a horse with more of a slender neck, especially on the underneath side. I want to see a short back, a low tail set, a lot of slope in the hip, and I want its hocks sitting as close to the ground as possible.

Although it's not true one hundred percent of the time, I think you stand a better chance of having a great athlete if those attributes are there. If a horse is just the opposite, it doesn't mean that horse can't be great, but the likelihood is slim. More often than not, what I've described is the best, but all horses are individuals. Some are easy to work with, some are high strung, some are laid back, and others are just numb and lazy.

With horses that are very timid, a small correction will mean a lot. There are other horses that a small correction doesn't mean anything to. It's the same as with children. Some kids can be scolded a little bit and it lasts for three weeks; others you can scold and they're laughing at you before you turn your back. Even a horse that is timid-minded and sensitive to the touch—if they are athletes, are smart, and are approached in the right way—can be some of the easiest horses to train. But if you get too tough on them or ask too much too fast, they can turn into the biggest mess you've ever seen.

On the contrary, a little bit duller horse that's not so sensitive will tolerate some mistakes and it won't make as much difference to them. They can still turn out to be really nice horses. Overall, training horses can be done on a punishment and reward system. You must try to make the wrong things really hard for them and the right things really easy, as Ray Hunt says. To me, that sums it up best.

If we don't keep learning, we're going to get passed up. That's just the bottom line. Sometimes you learn something new from a horse and sometimes from talking to or watching someone else. Often, you are only relearning something you had forgotten.

Reined cow horse competition has been around forever, but the sport has grown very quickly in the past few years. This competition combines three events: cutting, reining, and working a single cow down a fence. It's a difficult event to train for because the horse has to learn several things and become very good at three different disciplines. In the past, most people focused only on cutting or reining, but this combined event is becoming increasingly popular.

Although we enjoy training horses for a living, there is only so much money that can be made in training because of the costs and overhead. If I can get a horse trained nicely and compete in an event that pays well, that helps supplement my income.

Some of the victories I was most proud of are winning the World's Greatest Horseman Contest in 2003 and 2004. This competition includes four events: cutting, roping, reining, and working a cow down the fence. Only thirty or forty horses enter because there are so few horses that can do all

of those events at a winning level. It's hard for people to excel in that many events also, which makes it an exciting event.

Those two victories really stand out for me because I won them on two different horses. One of them was Cowgirls Are Smart, and the other was A Chic 'N Time. Both are by Smart Chic O'Lena. Both years when I left to go to that event, which was then held in Amarillo, I felt that if I was lucky enough and God was willing, I had a good enough horse to win. All I needed was a little luck and to do my job right.

The other competition I'm very proud of is winning the World's Richest Stock Horse Contest, a futurity for three-year-olds in California. The contest is much like the World's Greatest Horseman Contest without the roping. They opened it to only thirty horses last year, with a $5,000 entry fee and a $100,000 prize. I entered A Chic 'N Time; God was willing and we won it.

A Chic 'N Time is the father of a horse I own, Chromium Cowboy. He's a great horse that has won close to $160,000. Cowboy is a naturally good athlete and has a heart as big as the barn he lives in. He has a lot of try and a lot of will to please. This is what makes him a winner.

The horse show industry is going strong and is growing. There are increasingly more people, more horses, and more money involved. I believe horses are getting better as well. There are better bloodlines and better characteristics in horses than there were thirty years ago, and these bloodlines are giving show horses more talent and more intelligence.

We're riding nicer horses that are easier to train, but there is a downside. Throughout this process, the horses are not as sturdy as they were a few decades ago; they don't have as much bone in their legs. Although it's not direct line breeding like breeding a father to a daughter, they are inbred indirectly down the line. Everyone wants a winner, and there are certain sires that put certain characteristics into horses. But no matter what bloodlines you use, you have to have very strong mare power as well.

Training horses can be very frustrating, and it is difficult to maintain good horsemanship if an individual is prone to losing his temper. It's better to do things softer and easier with a horse when possible. As I said, my philosophy is to make the wrong things hard and the right things easy. That takes skilled horsemanship and a keen thought process. Good horsemanship goes right out the window if you lose your temper. You cannot think well when you're upset, and this leads to poor judgment. It's better to just keep riding and pulling and thinking your way through it.

This is not to say that there aren't horses you need to be a little bit tougher on, but if you just continue to do things as soft and as smart as possible, you can always get a little bit tougher tomorrow or the next day if you decide that is what will be required. Once you get angry and use poor judgment, you can't take it back. When you get too frustrated, it's best to go fix some fence or do something else.

If a young person wants to become a successful trainer, they must be ready to go through some lean times. Success also requires honesty and an impeccable work ethic. If a person has those things, I would suggest they find a trainer whose training style and finished product they like. Then try to be around that person, whether it's through taking lessons from them or going to work for them.

Horsemanship is a really big word. A good horseman is a person who is fair. Because they are animals, you have to meet them halfway and with fairness. You also must be open-minded to learning new things, and you must be able to take constructive criticism from someone who knows more than you do. I try to keep learning and getting better at what I do. No matter what level of success you reach, there will always be someone coming up who is a little hungrier and trying a little harder than you, and if you're not getting better, you will be passed up.

th, some are high strung, some are laid back, and others are just numb and lazy.

Because they are animals, you have to meet them halfway and with fairness.

Ray Hunt

Like his unique philosophies, Ray Hunt's contribution to American horsemanship over the past four decades is hard to sum up. His influence has spawned an approach to working with horses based on understanding and compassion rather than domination, and this approach has spread throughout the training world almost imperceptibly over several decades. Both horses and humans have benefited from Ray's influence.

Ray was raised on an Idaho farm where his father plowed, planted, and cut hay using draft horses. When Ray got older, he worked as a cowboy, riding rough stock for large outfits in northern Nevada. But living the cowboy life was not his ultimate calling. A disciple and colleague of the great horseman, Tom Dorrance, Ray has dedicated the last thirty-plus years to teaching people how to create a true partnership with the horse based on trust, respect, and understanding. As he often says, "I'm here for the horse, to help him get a better deal."

This wasn't always the case for Ray. As a young cowboy in the 1950s, he tried the more traditional approaches to training until a horse called Hondo changed everything. One winter, he was Ray's only ride, but the horse bucked, kicked, and bit

persistently. Although Ray had pity on the horse, he used all of the physical methods he knew of to bring him around. Nevertheless, things didn't get much better.

That winter of 1960-61, Ray took the colt to Tom Dorrance, who had had phenomenal success with unmanageable horses. Hondo was soon well-behaved whenever Tom worked with him, but when Ray was once again alone with the horse, his old behavior returned. He was determined to understand what caused the difference.

What Ray discovered was that the horse was afraid of him because he was still using too much force. His instinct told him this wasn't the right way. It was then, with Tom's coaching, that he learned and embraced a new way of working with horses. With a new approach, Hondo was soon as gentle, smooth, and pleasant to be around as any good horse. Ray says everything he now knows began with that horse.

A COMPASSIONATE APPROACH

Ray's understanding of the instincts, feelings, and mindset of the horse are at the heart of his approach to training. This knowledge didn't come easy. It took years of hard work, commitment, and genuine affection for the animal to become the revered horseman he is today. With the confidence that everything he does is in the best interest of the horse, Ray developed his widely-recognized philosophy, "Make the wrong thing difficult and the right thing easy."

In the early years, the approaches to horsemanship embraced by Tom Dorrance, Ray Hunt, and a few others was considered radical by old-time horsemen. "Breaking" a horse through domination had long been the protocol, and it was simply a necessary side-effect that the colt experienced panic and terror. Ray's approach, however, attempts to eliminate the horse's fear through patience and compassionate treatment.

Many times, this empathetic approach gets surprisingly quick results. In fact, to some observers, the responses Ray gets through his methods appear somewhat mystical. Although it may look like magic, there is less mystery to these abilities than there is patience and perseverance. Much of the secret to the way horses respond to Ray is his keen awareness of what the horse is communicating with each movement or expression. Such a skill can only be developed through years of experience, yet participants at Ray's five-day clinics walk away with much deeper knowledge of what the horse can tell us through its body language and behavior.

Ray does not train with a rulebook or formula. Nor are his methods about training for horseshows or particular events, although riders at any level and in any discipline can benefit

from his teachings. Through his lessons and by his example, Ray promotes the principles of awareness, compassion, generosity, discipline, wisdom, harmony, and patience.

SHARING THE KNOWLEDGE

Ray and his wife, Carolyn, are on the road frequently traveling across the United States and worldwide holding clinics. The clinics last five days. In the mornings, he works with green colts that have had little or no handling. In the afternoons, he holds horsemanship classes where he works with riders whose horses have been ridden fifteen times or more.

Through these clinics, Ray has started more than ten thousand colts. In a short time, even untouched colts accept being haltered, led, saddled, and ridden. By the end of the week, they have caught on to the basics of stopping, backing, and changing leads on command. One of the most exhilarating parts of Ray's clinics is that on the first day, the colts are ridden without bridles. Ray says this keeps the rider humble and makes it impossible for them to attempt to control the horse. This, he says, is the beginning of trust.

Ray doesn't talk to horses because he believes the horse feels the right communication without words. He does, however, offer many words of wisdom to his human students. "Make

your idea his idea. Fix it up and let him find it. Prepare to position for the transition. Do more by doing less. Don't try to be the boss. If the horse is right on his feet, he'll be right on his head." These are phrases that anyone who spends much time around Ray will become familiar with.

Where there is resistance, Ray works with a horse until the body becomes untroubled—whether this takes an hour or a few years to accomplish. Over and over, he preaches patience, respect, and understanding, because as well as he understands horses, he understands the human animal as well. He knows that fighting often comes more natural to our species than making peace.

WALKING THE TALK

Ray calls the horse his livelihood, his hobby, and his passion. "If given a little thought, a little understanding, and a little common sense, the horse gives back in full measure," he says. "The horse never ceases to amaze me with what he can get done with very little help from the human."

He believes pride often causes the human to make it a win or lose situation, while the horse doesn't know what a contest is until the human shows it to him. In contrast to people, Ray says that the horse is always honest and will tell you the facts.

Of course, no matter how much wisdom one has gained, good horsemanship requires hard work. "Practice doesn't make perfect. Perfect practice makes perfect," Ray often says. Working patiently with the horse, at his own pace with awareness and compassion instead of brutality, is perfect practice.

At the crux of Ray's teaching is understanding between horse and man, and this works both ways. As Ray exhorts, "Believe in your horse, so your horse can believe in you." It would be difficult to measure the influence Ray Hunt has had on horsemanship in this country and worldwide. Through his influence, the world is full of better horsemen and horsewomen. And more importantly, it is a safer and less frightening place for horses to exist.